Exploring DeepSeek-V3

A Comprehensive Guide to Leveraging Open-Source AI for Innovation and Efficiency

CONTENTS:

- Other Notable Models: Exploring different models and their use cases.

Chapter 3: Setting Up and Getting Started with DeepSeek

- How to access DeepSeek's models.
- Setting up DeepSeek on various platforms (iOS, Android, Web).
- Installation process for running DeepSeek locally.

Chapter 4: Working with DeepSeek Models

- Interacting with the models via the mobile app and web interface.
- Understanding how to prompt and use DeepSeek's AI for various tasks.
- Using DeepSeek in practical scenarios (e.g., content creation, customer support, data analysis).

Chapter 5: Advanced Features and Customization

- Customizing DeepSeek models to suit specific needs.
- Advanced settings and how to configure the models for your use case.
- Working with APIs for deeper integrations into existing software systems.

Chapter 6: DeepSeek-V3 for Developers

- How to integrate DeepSeek into applications using APIs.
- Using DeepSeek for machine learning and data analysis projects.
- Examples of coding projects with DeepSeek and potential open-source collaborations.

Chapter 7: Real-World Use Cases and Case Studies

- Case studies from industries benefiting from DeepSeek (e.g., healthcare, education, marketing).
- Exploring how businesses are using DeepSeek for productivity enhancements.
- Success stories and lessons learned from real-world applications.

Chapter 8: The Future of DeepSeek and AI

- The potential future developments for DeepSeek.
- How DeepSeek fits into the larger AI landscape.
- Emerging trends in AI and where DeepSeek is headed.

Chapter 9: Ethical Considerations and Data Privacy

- Exploring the ethical use of AI models.

- Understanding data privacy concerns and policies in using DeepSeek.
- Best practices for handling user data responsibly when interacting with DeepSeek models.

Chapter 10: Troubleshooting and Common Issues

- Common problems users face and how to resolve them.
- Optimizing performance for different environments.
- Community support and where to find help.

CHAPTER 11: DeepSeek-V3: The Next Evolution in AI Technology

- Introduction to Scaling DeepSeek-V3
- Cloud-based Deployment
- Distributed Computing with DeepSeek-V3
- Performance Tuning and Optimization

CHAPTER 12: How to Install and Run DeepSeek-V3

- Step 1: Downloading DeepSeek-V3
- Step 2: Running DeepSeek-V3 Locally
- Step 3: Integrating DeepSeek-V3 into Your Applications
- Step 4: Cloud-Based Deployment (Optional)

- Troubleshooting

Conclusion

- Recap of the key takeaways about DeepSeek.
- Encouraging continued exploration of open-source AI tools.
- Final thoughts on the impact of DeepSeek and similar AI innovations on the future of work and technology.

Appendices

- A1: How to install and run DeepSeek-R1 on different platforms.
- A2: Glossary of AI-related terms.
- A3: Resources for further learning (e.g., links to tutorials, forums, and communities).

Exploring DeepSeek

A Comprehensive Guide to Leveraging Open-Source AI for Innovation and Efficiency

Introduction

Overview of DeepSeek and Its Rise in the AI Industry

DeepSeek is quickly emerging as a powerful player in the world of artificial intelligence, offering cutting-edge models that rival some of the biggest names in AI. Founded in 2023, DeepSeek has made a name for itself by providing advanced, open-source AI models with remarkable capabilities in natural language processing, multimodal understanding, and efficient performance. DeepSeek's models, including the well-known DeepSeek-R1 and the last version DeepSeek-V3 are paving the way for more accessible and affordable AI solutions for businesses and developers.

Importance of Open-Source AI Models and the Benefits of Using Them

Open-source AI represents a paradigm shift in how we build and deploy artificial intelligence. By providing free access to its powerful models, DeepSeek enables users to customize and implement these tools in a variety of use cases, from content creation to data analysis. The benefits of using open-source AI models like DeepSeek include lower development costs, greater flexibility, and a collaborative ecosystem that fosters innovation. With DeepSeek, users can contribute to the future of AI, refine existing models, and create new solutions based on open standards.

Purpose of the Book: A Guide to Understanding and Leveraging DeepSeek

This book is designed to serve as a comprehensive guide to mastering DeepSeek's open-source AI models. Whether you're a developer looking to integrate DeepSeek into your applications, a business owner seeking to leverage AI for greater efficiency, or simply an AI enthusiast curious about the possibilities of open-source AI, this book will provide you with the tools and knowledge you need to get started. We'll explore the key features, installation steps, real-world applications, and future trends in AI, empowering you to harness the full potential of DeepSeek for your projects.

Chapter 1: What is DeepSeek?

History and Background of DeepSeek

DeepSeek was founded in 2023 as a cutting-edge artificial intelligence company that quickly gained attention for its remarkable innovations in the field of machine learning and natural language processing. The company's mission is to provide accessible, high-performance AI models while reducing the cost and complexity typically associated with advanced AI technologies. DeepSeek was built with the goal of bridging the gap between powerful AI models and widespread, practical applications across various industries.

With the AI space becoming increasingly competitive, DeepSeek has emerged as a fresh challenger, offering an open-source approach that gives developers and businesses the freedom to integrate and customize AI tools to suit their specific needs. The company has garnered support from the global AI community by releasing its models under open-source licenses, which allows anyone to contribute, adapt, and improve upon its technology.

Key Founders and Their Vision for the Company

The founders of DeepSeek, led by CEO Liang Wenfeng, are visionaries in the world of artificial intelligence. Wenfeng and his team have extensive backgrounds in machine learning, natural language processing, and deep learning. Their combined expertise in these areas has enabled DeepSeek to rapidly develop sophisticated AI models while ensuring they remain accessible and usable by a broad audience.

Wenfeng's vision for DeepSeek is centered on democratizing artificial intelligence and making it available to all, from independent developers to large enterprises. By fostering an open-source culture, DeepSeek aims to empower individuals and organizations to build on top of its technology and create innovative AI-driven solutions. The company also focuses on creating models that are not only cutting-edge but also cost-efficient, allowing businesses to integrate AI without breaking the bank.

What Makes DeepSeek Different from Other AI Models?

DeepSeek stands out in several key areas when compared to other AI models available on the market:

1. **Cost-Efficiency:** One of the major advantages of DeepSeek's AI models is their cost efficiency. While developing high-performance AI models like GPT-4 can cost millions of dollars, DeepSeek has been able to develop its models with a fraction of that investment. For example, DeepSeek's flagship model, DeepSeek-R1, was trained for around $6 million, significantly lower than the estimated $100 million for training similar models. This makes DeepSeek an attractive option for startups, researchers, and businesses looking for advanced AI without the exorbitant price tag.
2. **Efficiency and Performance:** DeepSeek has invested heavily in optimizing its models for efficiency. Their AI systems not only provide accurate results but do so faster and using fewer computational resources than many of their competitors. This makes DeepSeek ideal for users who require high performance without needing to invest in large-scale infrastructure.
3. **Open-Source Nature:** Unlike proprietary AI models like OpenAI's GPT series, DeepSeek offers open-source access to its models, enabling developers to download, modify, and deploy them freely. This fosters a collaborative environment where the AI community can contribute to the development and refinement of DeepSeek's

models. The open-source nature also allows businesses to adapt the models to fit their specific needs, ensuring greater flexibility and control over their AI projects.

4. **Multimodal Capabilities:** Another unique feature of DeepSeek is its ability to handle both text and visual information in a single model. The DeepSeek-VL model, for example, is designed to understand images alongside text, which sets it apart from many traditional AI models that focus solely on text-based tasks. This multimodal approach expands the range of tasks DeepSeek can perform, making it useful for applications in areas such as content generation, data analysis, and customer service.

Conclusion

DeepSeek is reshaping the AI landscape by offering powerful, efficient, and open-source models that are accessible to a broad audience. Its commitment to reducing the cost of AI development while maintaining high performance sets it apart from its competitors. With its open-source framework, DeepSeek invites collaboration and innovation, making it a valuable tool for developers, businesses, and AI enthusiasts alike.

Chapter 2: Key Features of DeepSeek Models

DeepSeek offers a diverse range of advanced AI models designed to tackle a wide variety of tasks, from natural language processing (NLP) to image recognition. In this chapter, we will dive deep into the key models developed by DeepSeek, including their core features, capabilities, and applications. By understanding these models, you'll be equipped with the knowledge to utilize them effectively in your projects.

DeepSeek-R1 Model: Introduction and Capabilities

The **DeepSeek-R1** model is the cornerstone of DeepSeek's AI offerings, providing cutting-edge performance in natural language understanding and generation. It is designed to handle a range of text-based tasks such as writing assistance, customer support automation, content generation, and much more.

Key Features and Capabilities:

- **Natural Language Processing (NLP):** DeepSeek-R1 excels in text-based tasks, from generating human-like content to interpreting and summarizing lengthy documents. It can assist in content creation, translation, sentiment analysis, and chatbot interactions.

- **Speed and Efficiency:** Unlike other models in its class, DeepSeek-R1 was trained with efficiency in mind. It produces fast results without consuming excessive computational resources, making it ideal for both small-scale applications and large enterprise solutions.
- **Contextual Understanding:** One of the standout features of DeepSeek-R1 is its ability to understand context in conversations. Whether it's answering customer queries, drafting emails, or providing insights, DeepSeek-R1 considers the entire context of the conversation, providing more relevant and coherent responses.
- **Training on Diverse Datasets:** Trained on a broad and diverse dataset, DeepSeek-R1 is adaptable to various industries and use cases. It can quickly learn and understand new terms, jargon, and industry-specific language, making it versatile across fields like marketing, finance, healthcare, and education.

Applications:

- **Content Creation:** DeepSeek-R1 can generate articles, blog posts, and product descriptions, providing businesses with high-quality content at scale.

- **Customer Support:** Used in chatbots and virtual assistants, it can resolve customer inquiries and provide support around the clock.
- **Sentiment Analysis:** Businesses can use DeepSeek-R1 to analyze customer feedback and gauge public sentiment about their products or services.

DeepSeek-VL Model: Multimodal Capabilities and Applications

The **DeepSeek-VL** model takes AI a step further by offering multimodal capabilities, meaning it can process both visual (image) and textual information. This versatility enables the DeepSeek-VL model to handle a wider range of tasks that involve images, videos, and text, making it a powerful tool for industries that require image recognition and language comprehension in tandem.

Key Features and Capabilities:

- **Image Recognition:** DeepSeek-VL is equipped with advanced image processing algorithms that can recognize and classify images with high accuracy. Whether it's identifying objects in photos or understanding the context behind a visual scene, DeepSeek-VL can provide detailed analysis of images.

- **Text-to-Image and Image-to-Text:** One of the most powerful features of DeepSeek-VL is its ability to generate textual descriptions from images (image-to-text) and create images based on textual descriptions (text-to-image). This makes it an invaluable tool for applications in digital media, marketing, and education.
- **Visual Question Answering (VQA):** DeepSeek-VL can answer questions related to the content of an image. This feature is ideal for interactive applications that need to provide insights based on visual data, such as image search engines or educational tools.
- **Multimodal Content Creation:** With DeepSeek-VL, users can create content that combines both text and visual elements seamlessly. For example, the model can assist in designing marketing materials, generating infographics, or even creating interactive learning modules.

Applications:

- **E-commerce and Retail:** DeepSeek-VL can analyze product images and generate detailed descriptions, helping retailers automate product listings and improve search functionality.

- **Medical Imaging:** In healthcare, DeepSeek-VL can be used to interpret medical images (such as X-rays or MRIs) alongside text reports, making it easier for medical professionals to get insights from both visual and textual data.
- **Education and Training:** The ability to create educational content that combines images with explanatory text allows DeepSeek-VL to be used in interactive training programs, textbooks, and online courses.

Other Notable Models: Exploring Different Models and Their Use Cases

Beyond the flagship **DeepSeek-R1** and **DeepSeek-VL**, the company offers several other specialized models tailored for various use cases.

1. DeepSeek-LM (Language Model)

- **Purpose:** DeepSeek-LM is designed for applications that require deep linguistic understanding, such as language translation, summarization, and grammar correction.

- **Use Case:** It can be used in customer support tools that handle multilingual queries or in content management systems to automatically summarize long-form content.

2. DeepSeek-DS (Data Science Model)

- **Purpose:** DeepSeek-DS is focused on data analysis and prediction tasks, equipped with machine learning capabilities to process large datasets and provide valuable insights.
- **Use Case:** Businesses can use DeepSeek-DS to analyze sales data, predict trends, and optimize inventory management.

3. DeepSeek-SM (Speech Model)

- **Purpose:** DeepSeek-SM specializes in speech recognition and synthesis, enabling applications that require voice interactions, like virtual assistants or transcription services.
- **Use Case:** It can be used in healthcare systems for transcribing patient records or in voice-activated smart devices.

4. DeepSeek-ER (Entity Recognition Model)

- **Purpose:** This model is trained to identify and categorize entities within unstructured text, such as names, dates, locations, and more.

- **Use Case:** It's ideal for applications in legal document analysis, where extracting key entities from contracts is crucial, or in customer service chatbots that need to understand user inputs.

Conclusion

The DeepSeek suite of models represents a diverse and robust toolkit for solving a wide range of problems, from simple text generation to advanced multimodal tasks involving both text and images. The flagship **DeepSeek-R1** model provides unmatched efficiency for text-based applications, while **DeepSeek-VL** opens new doors for industries looking to merge visual and textual data for deeper insights and more creative applications. Additionally, the other specialized models cater to specific needs such as data analysis, speech recognition, and entity extraction, making DeepSeek a versatile and highly effective solution for developers and businesses across various sectors.

In the next chapter, we will explore how to set up and get started with DeepSeek, so you can start harnessing the power of these models in your own projects.

Chapter 3: Setting Up and Getting Started with DeepSeek

DeepSeek's powerful AI models are designed to be easy to access and integrate into a variety of platforms. Whether you're a developer looking to run DeepSeek locally, a business wanting to integrate it into your web application, or an individual exploring its mobile applications, this chapter will walk you through the steps needed to get started with DeepSeek across different platforms.

How to Access DeepSeek's Models

Accessing DeepSeek's models is straightforward. As an open-source AI company, DeepSeek provides a range of options for developers and businesses to utilize its models in their projects. You can start using DeepSeek's models by following these steps:

1. Official Website & Open-Source Repository

- **Website Access:** Visit DeepSeek's official website (www.deepseek.ai) to learn more about the available models, their features, and their use cases. You can find detailed documentation and API access information here.

- **GitHub Repository:** DeepSeek hosts its open-source models on GitHub. To access and contribute to DeepSeek's models, go to the DeepSeek GitHub page (https://github.com/DeepSeek) and clone the repositories of your desired models. The repository contains installation guides, configuration files, and model details.

2. API Access

- For users who prefer not to run the models locally, DeepSeek also offers API access to its models. You can sign up for an API key on their website, and once you have the key, you can start making requests to their server-based models.
- The API provides a simple way to integrate DeepSeek's capabilities into your applications without needing to manage complex infrastructure or hardware requirements.

Setting Up DeepSeek on Various Platforms (iOS, Android, Web)

DeepSeek has made its models available across a wide range of platforms, ensuring users can easily access them regardless of their device type. Here's how to get started on each platform:

1. iOS (Mobile Application) DeepSeek has released 'an official mobile application for iOS devices. This app allows users to access a wide range of DeepSeek's capabilities right from their iPhones or iPads.

- **Step 1:** Visit the **App Store** on your iOS device.
- **Step 2:** Search for "DeepSeek" and download the official app.
- **Step 3:** Open the app and sign in with your DeepSeek account or create a new account if you don't have one.
- **Step 4:** Once logged in, you can begin exploring DeepSeek's capabilities, from text-based interactions to image recognition, depending on the model you choose to use.

The iOS app is designed to be intuitive and user-friendly, offering easy access to features like voice commands, text generation, and visual recognition.

---

2. Android (Mobile Application) DeepSeek also provides an official app for Android users, allowing access to the same powerful AI models on your mobile device.

- **Step 1:** Go to the **Google Play Store** on your Android device.
- **Step 2:** Search for "DeepSeek" and select the app from the search results.
- **Step 3:** Tap "Install" to download the app to your device.
- **Step 4:** Open the app and log in to your DeepSeek account, or sign up for a new account if necessary.
- **Step 5:** Once set up, you can start using the app for tasks such as natural language processing, text generation, and even multimodal tasks involving images.

The Android app mirrors the functionality of the iOS app, allowing you to take DeepSeek's AI on the go for both personal and professional use.

---

3. Web Access (Browser-Based Platform)
DeepSeek's web platform allows users to interact with the models via a browser, providing flexibility for those who prefer working on their desktop or laptop.

- **Step 1:** Open a web browser and go to DeepSeek's official website (www.deepseek.ai).
- **Step 2:** Sign up for a free account or log in if you already have one.

- **Step 3:** From the dashboard, you can choose from a list of available models, such as DeepSeek-R1 or DeepSeek-VL, and begin exploring their capabilities directly through the web interface.

The web platform is designed to be responsive and compatible with most modern browsers, ensuring a seamless experience across devices.

Installation Process for Running DeepSeek Locally

For developers or organizations who prefer to run DeepSeek's models locally, the process is relatively straightforward, though it may require some technical expertise. Here's a step-by-step guide to running DeepSeek locally:

---

1. Prerequisites Before installing DeepSeek locally, make sure your system meets the following requirements:

- **Operating System:** Linux (Ubuntu or similar), macOS, or Windows (via WSL for Linux compatibility).
- **Python Version:** Python 3.7 or higher.

- **RAM:** At least 16GB of RAM (more may be needed for large models).
- **Disk Space:** 50GB of free disk space or more (depending on the model).
- **Dependencies:** Docker (recommended for easy setup) or direct installation via pip and Git.

---

2. Cloning the Repository To begin, you will need to clone the DeepSeek repository from GitHub.

- **Step 1:** Open a terminal and clone the DeepSeek repository:

  bash

  git clone https://github.com/DeepSeek/DeepSeek.git

- **Step 2:** Navigate to the directory where the repository was cloned:

  bash

  cd DeepSeek

---

3. Installing Dependencies

- **Step 1:** If using Docker, build the Docker image:

  bash

  docker build -t deepseek .

- **Step 2:** Alternatively, if you prefer to install directly via pip, use the following commands:

  bash

  pip install -r requirements.txt

This will install all necessary dependencies, including TensorFlow, PyTorch, and other essential libraries.

---

4. Running DeepSeek Locally Once the dependencies are installed, you can run DeepSeek models locally. Here's how to start the model:

- **Step 1:** Navigate to the model directory you want to run (for example, DeepSeek-R1).
- **Step 2:** Start the model using the following command:

```bash
python run_model.py
```

- **Step 3:** The model will initialize, and you can begin interacting with it directly from your terminal or through a local API endpoint.

---

5. Using a Local API (Optional) For more advanced users, you can expose DeepSeek's models via a local API, allowing you to integrate them into your applications seamlessly.

- **Step 1:** Start the local server:

```bash
python api_server.py
```

- **Step 2:** You can now make API requests to interact with the model, just as you would when using the cloud-based API.

Conclusion

Getting started with DeepSeek is easy, whether you're using its mobile apps, web interface, or running it locally. The process is designed to be accessible to both technical and non-technical users. By following the steps in this chapter, you can begin harnessing the power of DeepSeek's AI models for your projects, unlocking new capabilities in natural language processing, image recognition, and multimodal applications. In the next chapter, we will explore practical examples and use cases, helping you get the most out of DeepSeek's features.

Chapter 4: Working with DeepSeek Models

In this chapter, we will explore how to effectively interact with DeepSeek's AI models, understand how to prompt the models for various tasks, and use DeepSeek's capabilities in practical scenarios. Whether you're using DeepSeek through its mobile app, web interface, or API, this chapter will guide you through the essentials to maximize your experience with the platform.

Interacting with the Models via the Mobile App and Web Interface

DeepSeek's mobile app and web interface offer user-friendly environments to interact with its powerful AI models. These platforms are designed to make it easy for both beginners and advanced users to access DeepSeek's capabilities.

---

1. Mobile App Interface

- **Step 1:** Open the DeepSeek app on your mobile device (available for iOS and Android).
- **Step 2:** Log in to your account (or sign up if you're a new user).

- **Step 3:** Once logged in, you will see the list of available models (e.g., DeepSeek-R1, DeepSeek-VL). You can select a model based on your needs.
- **Step 4:** You can interact with the model by typing prompts in the text input box or by speaking your query if voice input is enabled.

The mobile app allows you to use DeepSeek's models in various scenarios, from generating text content to processing images. It's optimized for on-the-go use, so you can access DeepSeek's features anytime, anywhere.

---

2. Web Interface

- **Step 1:** Open a browser and navigate to DeepSeek's official website (www.deepseek.ai).
- **Step 2:** Log in to your DeepSeek account or create a new one.
- **Step 3:** From the dashboard, you'll have access to the different models and tools offered by DeepSeek. You can choose to interact with text-based models or multimodal models like DeepSeek-VL.
- **Step 4:** You can enter your prompts in the provided text box or use the drag-and-drop

feature to upload images for image-related tasks.

The web interface offers a more robust and feature-rich environment, allowing you to access advanced settings, manage API keys, and run multiple models simultaneously. It's ideal for users who want more control and functionality than the mobile app offers.

Understanding How to Prompt and Use DeepSeek's AI for Various Tasks

DeepSeek's AI models are highly versatile, allowing you to use them for a variety of tasks. To get the best results, it's important to know how to craft your prompts effectively. Below are tips for prompting DeepSeek's models to achieve desired outcomes.

---

1. Text-Based Tasks (e.g., Content Creation, Data Analysis)

- **Content Creation:** DeepSeek excels in content generation tasks, such as writing articles, blog posts, product descriptions, and more.

    - **Prompt Example for Content Creation:** "Write a 500-word article about the benefits of deep learning in healthcare."
    - **Tips:** Be clear and specific with your request. Include key points you'd like the AI to cover (e.g., benefits, examples, challenges).
- **Customer Support:** Use DeepSeek to create automated customer support responses or FAQs.
    - **Prompt Example for Customer Support:** "Generate a response for a customer asking how to return an item."
    - **Tips:** Specify the tone of the response (e.g., friendly, professional) and the type of interaction (e.g., product returns, shipping inquiries).
- **Data Analysis and Summarization:** DeepSeek's AI can help summarize long documents, analyze datasets, and generate insights.
    - **Prompt Example for Data Analysis:** "Summarize the key findings of this dataset: [insert dataset]."
    - **Tips:** Make sure to provide sufficient context and include any specific aspects you want the model to focus on (e.g., trends, outliers).

---

2. Image-Related Tasks (e.g., DeepSeek-VL Model)

DeepSeek's multimodal models like **DeepSeek-VL** can process images in addition to text, making them highly useful for a wide variety of image-based tasks such as object recognition, image captioning, and visual content generation.

- **Prompt Example for Image Captioning:** "Generate a descriptive caption for this image of a sunset over the ocean."
    - **Tips:** Be specific about what aspects of the image you want to highlight (e.g., the mood, location, or key elements of the image).
- **Prompt Example for Image Recognition:** "Identify objects and provide a detailed analysis of the content in this photo."
    - **Tips:** If you're working with complex images, it's helpful to provide additional instructions on what to look for (e.g., "highlight animals, people, or landmarks in the image").

Using DeepSeek in Practical Scenarios

DeepSeek's models can be applied across various domains, offering innovative solutions for both individuals and businesses. Below are some common practical use cases and examples of how you can leverage DeepSeek in different scenarios.

---

1. Content Creation for Blogs and Social Media

DeepSeek's AI models can be your creative partner in generating high-quality written content. Whether you need blog posts, social media captions, or even video scripts, DeepSeek can handle it all.

- **Example:** A blogger can use DeepSeek to generate daily posts on topics like tech news, lifestyle tips, or product reviews. Simply provide the desired subject and tone, and DeepSeek will generate engaging, relevant content.

---

2. Customer Support Automation

DeepSeek is an excellent tool for automating customer support services. By integrating DeepSeek's models into your customer service channels, you can quickly generate responses to common customer queries, provide instant support, and even handle complicated cases through AI-powered interactions.

- **Example:** A small business can integrate DeepSeek into its chatbot system, allowing customers to ask questions about product features, shipping policies, or troubleshooting. DeepSeek can respond instantly with accurate, context-aware answers, reducing the need for live agents.

---

3. Data Analysis and Reporting

DeepSeek's natural language processing (NLP) capabilities can help you analyze large datasets, identify trends, and summarize key findings. This is particularly useful for businesses that need to digest vast amounts of data and create concise reports.

- **Example:** A financial analyst can use DeepSeek to analyze stock performance data and generate a summary report on market trends and predictions. You can also upload CSV files or raw data for the model to process and summarize.

---

4. Personal Assistants and Productivity Tools

DeepSeek can serve as an AI-powered personal assistant to help you stay organized, manage tasks, and even suggest improvements to your workflow. You can prompt DeepSeek to generate reminders, set up schedules, or help brainstorm new ideas for your projects.

- **Example:** A project manager can use DeepSeek to generate project timelines, set reminders for deadlines, and even draft communication for team members. Simply prompt DeepSeek with project details, and it will create a comprehensive task plan.

---

5. Creative Work (Art, Music, and Design)

DeepSeek's multimodal AI models can be used in creative industries for generating art, music, and even design layouts. Artists and designers can use DeepSeek to explore new ideas, create variations, or generate entirely new pieces of work.

- **Example:** A graphic designer can use DeepSeek to generate initial design concepts based on a given theme or brief. Artists can also use DeepSeek to experiment with different styles or create concept art for video games, animations, or illustrations.

Conclusion

By understanding how to interact with DeepSeek's models and crafting precise prompts, you can unlock the full potential of the platform for a variety of tasks. From content creation to customer support and data analysis, DeepSeek's capabilities can be leveraged to streamline workflows, boost productivity, and innovate across industries. In the next chapter, we will dive deeper into integrating DeepSeek into your applications and scaling its use across different business needs.

Chapter 5: Advanced Features and Customization

In this chapter, we'll explore the advanced features of DeepSeek, focusing on how to customize the models to better suit your specific needs. We'll also cover the advanced settings and how to configure these models for various use cases. Finally, we'll dive into working with DeepSeek's APIs for deeper integrations into your existing software systems. These capabilities are designed for users who want to tailor DeepSeek's power and flexibility for more complex applications.

Customizing DeepSeek Models to Suit Specific Needs

One of the greatest strengths of DeepSeek is its adaptability. You can customize the models to suit your specific requirements, allowing you to tailor outputs, integrate them into workflows, or even fine-tune their behavior to achieve better results.

---

1. Fine-Tuning Models for Specific Domains

- **Why Fine-Tuning Matters:** While DeepSeek's pre-trained models are powerful out of the box, you may need them to perform better in a specific domain. Fine-tuning involves retraining the models with domain-specific data, helping them understand the nuances of your industry or use case.

- **Example Use Case:** If you're running a customer support chatbot for a medical clinic, you might want to fine-tune DeepSeek's AI to better understand medical terminology and provide more accurate responses for health-related queries.
- **How to Fine-Tune:** DeepSeek allows users to upload custom datasets to help fine-tune models. These datasets could include relevant documents, FAQs, or historical data that reflect the specific vocabulary and context of your domain.

---

2. Tailoring Responses Based on User Preferences

- **Response Personalization:** You can customize how DeepSeek responds to users by adjusting its tone, style, and level of detail. This is especially useful for businesses that want to ensure their AI-powered assistant communicates in a way that aligns with their brand voice.

- **Example Use Case:** A luxury brand might prefer a formal, polished tone, while a tech startup might opt for a casual, friendly voice. By fine-tuning response styles, you can ensure the AI fits seamlessly into your brand identity.

---

3. Training Custom Behavior with Reinforcement Learning

- **Custom Behavior Training:** If you want DeepSeek to perform specific tasks in a very particular way (such as maintaining conversation flow in a chatbot or prioritizing certain types of data analysis), reinforcement learning can be a valuable tool.
- **How It Works:** You can create a feedback loop where DeepSeek learns from interactions and adjusts its output based on positive or negative feedback. Over time, the model becomes increasingly attuned to your needs.

Advanced Settings and How to Configure the Models for Your Use Case

DeepSeek models come with a range of advanced settings that allow you to configure their behavior and output according to your specific requirements.

---

1. Adjusting Model Parameters

- **Temperature:** The "temperature" setting controls the randomness of the model's outputs. A higher temperature value (e.g., 0.7 or 0.8) will make the model more creative, generating responses that are less predictable. A lower temperature (e.g., 0.2 or 0.3) will result in more conservative and focused answers.
- **Max Tokens:** This parameter limits the length of the model's responses. By adjusting this setting, you can control whether the AI provides short, concise answers or longer, more detailed ones.
- **Example Use Case:** If you're building a customer service chatbot, you might set the temperature low to ensure responses are direct and to the point, while adjusting the max tokens to allow for more detailed replies when necessary.

2. Customizing Output Style and Format

- **Structured Outputs:** For use cases like generating reports, summaries, or data analysis, you may want to customize the output format. DeepSeek allows you to specify formats like bullet points, tables, or even code snippets depending on your needs.
- **Example Use Case:** If you're using DeepSeek for technical content generation, you could set the model to output information in a structured format (e.g., Markdown or LaTeX) to make the content easily editable and professional.

3. Configuring Workflow Automations

- **Automated Task Flows:** For more complex integrations, you can set up workflows that trigger specific actions when certain criteria are met. For example, you might configure DeepSeek to send email notifications when a certain keyword is mentioned in a customer query or when a specific report is generated.
- **Example Use Case:** For a marketing team, you could automate the creation of blog

posts or social media captions. When a new product launch occurs, DeepSeek can automatically generate content in the predefined format and post it according to your schedule.

Working with APIs for Deeper Integrations into Existing Software Systems

While DeepSeek offers an intuitive interface for basic tasks, the real power comes when you start integrating its models into your own software systems. DeepSeek provides robust APIs for deeper integrations, allowing you to build custom applications, automate workflows, and add AI capabilities to existing platforms.

---

1. Getting Started with DeepSeek's API

- **API Access:** To use DeepSeek's API, you'll first need to create an API key from your account dashboard. This key grants access to the model's functionality through HTTP requests.
- **API Documentation:** DeepSeek provides comprehensive API documentation, which outlines how to authenticate requests, call specific models, and handle responses. The

documentation includes example code snippets and tutorials to help you get started.

---

2. Integrating DeepSeek with CRM Systems

- **CRM Integration:** Many businesses rely on customer relationship management (CRM) systems to track interactions and manage customer data. With DeepSeek's API, you can integrate its capabilities directly into your CRM to automate lead scoring, analyze customer sentiment, or even generate personalized email responses based on customer profiles.
- **Example Use Case:** A sales team could use DeepSeek to analyze customer emails and automatically categorize them based on urgency, sentiment, or potential for conversion, streamlining the follow-up process.

---

3. Building Custom Applications

- **Building with DeepSeek:** If you have specific business needs or are developing a product that could benefit from AI-powered functionality, you can use DeepSeek's API to create custom applications. Whether you're developing a mobile app, website, or SaaS platform, integrating DeepSeek can help enhance the user experience with advanced AI features.

- **Example Use Case:** A mobile app focused on education could integrate DeepSeek to offer intelligent tutoring services, where the AI provides real-time feedback, suggests resources, and generates personalized study plans for users.

---

4. Automating Complex Business Workflows

- **Automation with APIs:** You can use DeepSeek's API to create end-to-end automation workflows. For example, when a customer places an order through an eCommerce platform, DeepSeek could automatically generate a personalized order confirmation email, update the CRM, and trigger follow-up actions based on the customer's previous interactions.
- **Example Use Case:** For an eCommerce business, DeepSeek's API could automate customer support responses, generate product recommendations, and even analyze purchase patterns to predict future trends.

Conclusion

DeepSeek offers a variety of advanced features that allow you to tailor its models to fit your specific needs. Whether you are fine-tuning models for specialized use cases, configuring advanced settings for optimal performance, or leveraging APIs for deep integrations, the platform is designed to be highly adaptable.

Chapter 6: DeepSeek for Developers

This chapter focuses on how developers can harness the power of DeepSeek for a variety of applications, including machine learning, data analysis, and coding projects. We will explore how to integrate DeepSeek into custom applications using its APIs, leverage its features for advanced data processing, and highlight potential open-source collaborations for those looking to extend DeepSeek's capabilities.

How to Integrate DeepSeek into Applications Using APIs

DeepSeek's robust API enables seamless integration with your existing software applications. By using these APIs, developers can unlock the full potential of DeepSeek, enabling a wide range of functionalities such as natural language processing, data generation, and automation. Let's break down the integration process and how you can use DeepSeek to enhance your applications.

---

1. Accessing DeepSeek's API

Before you start integrating, you need to access the DeepSeek API by creating an account and generating an API key. This key will be used for authenticating requests made to the API.

- **Steps to Access the API:**
  - Create a DeepSeek account.
  - Generate an API key from your dashboard.
  - Install the required libraries (DeepSeek SDK or other dependencies based on your programming language).
  - Begin sending authenticated API requests.

---

2. Sending API Requests

DeepSeek's API is based on RESTful architecture, making it easy to send requests and receive responses in JSON format. Here's how you can integrate DeepSeek into your application:

- **Make API Requests:**
  - Use HTTP methods (GET, POST, etc.) to send data to DeepSeek's endpoints.

- Structure your requests to include model parameters, data inputs, and any other necessary details (e.g., temperature, max tokens).

- **Example Request in Python:**

```
python
import requests

# Define the endpoint and API key
api_url = "https://api.deepseek.ai/v1/query"
headers = {
  "Authorization": "Bearer YOUR_API_KEY"
}

# Data to be sent to the API
data = {
  "model": "deepseek-r1",
  "query": "What are the latest AI trends in 2025?"
}

# Send the API request
response = requests.post(api_url, headers=headers, json=data)

# Print the response
print(response.json())
```

This will allow you to retrieve AI-generated responses directly within your application.

3. Handling API Responses

After sending a request, you'll receive a response containing the model's output. Responses typically include the results of the query, along with any relevant metadata like tokens used and processing time.

- **Example Response:**

json

```json
{
  "status": "success",
  "data": {
    "response": "The top AI trends for 2025 include advancements in natural language processing, quantum computing, and AI-powered automation."
  },
  "meta": {
    "tokens_used": 35,
    "processing_time": 0.7
  }
}
```

You can now parse this response to display results in your app or use the data for further analysis.

4. Error Handling

It's essential to manage errors gracefully to ensure a seamless user experience. If the API request fails (due to an invalid API key, incorrect input, or other issues), DeepSeek will provide error messages.

- **Example Error Response:**

json

```json
{
  "status": "error",
  "message": "Invalid API key. Please check your credentials."
}
```

Ensure that your application checks for errors and provides users with helpful messages when needed.

Using DeepSeek for Machine Learning and Data Analysis Projects

DeepSeek's models can be a valuable tool for machine learning and data analysis projects, thanks to its powerful natural language processing and data generation capabilities. Whether you're building an AI-based application, working with big data, or looking to enhance your

ML models, DeepSeek can assist in a variety of ways.

---

1. Leveraging DeepSeek for Data Preprocessing

Machine learning models rely heavily on quality data. DeepSeek can help preprocess data for training by generating synthetic datasets, summarizing large datasets, or even cleaning data.

- **Example Use Case:** For sentiment analysis projects, you can use DeepSeek to preprocess and annotate text data automatically, helping your model better understand the context.

---

2. Integrating DeepSeek for Feature Engineering

DeepSeek can also assist in feature engineering—creating new variables that will improve the performance of machine learning models. By generating new features based on text inputs, DeepSeek can help extract valuable insights that might not be immediately apparent.

- **Example Use Case:** If you're building a recommendation engine, you can use DeepSeek to generate embeddings or feature vectors for text-based products, which can then be used as input features for your machine learning model.

---

3. Automating Data Analysis with DeepSeek

You can use DeepSeek's AI models to automatically analyze large datasets, extracting insights, trends, or anomalies. For instance, DeepSeek can summarize research papers, identify key insights in text-heavy reports, or even generate structured summaries for review.

- **Example Use Case:** In financial analysis, DeepSeek can be used to scan through quarterly reports and summarize financial trends, allowing analysts to focus on critical insights instead of manually reading each document.

Examples of Coding Projects with DeepSeek and Potential Open-Source Collaborations

DeepSeek is an open-source AI platform, meaning developers can contribute to its ongoing development or build custom solutions. Here are a few coding project ideas that can be created using DeepSeek:

---

1. AI-Powered Chatbots for Customer Service

Building a chatbot that understands natural language and provides intelligent responses is one of the most common applications of DeepSeek. By integrating DeepSeek's models, you can create chatbots capable of handling customer inquiries, assisting with technical support, and generating FAQs dynamically.

- **Open-Source Collaboration Opportunity:** Contribute to an open-source repository where developers collaborate to fine-tune DeepSeek models for different industries or languages.

---

2. Intelligent Content Generation Tool

DeepSeek can be used to automatically generate content for blogs, social media posts, or product descriptions. By leveraging its ability to understand context and generate relevant text, you can develop a tool that automatically creates high-quality content based on user inputs.

- **Open-Source Collaboration Opportunity:** Work with others to create an open-source tool that integrates DeepSeek with CMS platforms or website builders, streamlining content creation for digital marketers.

---

3. Data Augmentation for ML Projects

For machine learning models that require large labeled datasets, DeepSeek can generate synthetic data to augment training datasets. This is especially useful in industries like healthcare or finance, where obtaining large labeled datasets can be difficult.

- **Open-Source Collaboration Opportunity:** Collaborate with researchers and data scientists on creating open-source repositories that offer data augmentation tools using DeepSeek's AI models for various domains.

4. Research Assistant for Academics

For academics working on research papers, DeepSeek can assist by summarizing articles, suggesting relevant literature, or even drafting portions of research papers based on given topics. This tool can be developed as an open-source solution for researchers.

- **Open-Source Collaboration Opportunity:** Contribute to an open-source research assistant tool that integrates DeepSeek for scientific papers, making it easier for researchers to stay up-to-date with the latest findings.

Conclusion

In this chapter, we've covered how developers can leverage DeepSeek to build powerful applications, automate data analysis, and contribute to open-source projects. From integrating DeepSeek into APIs to using it for machine learning, data processing, and content generation, the possibilities are vast. As a developer, embracing DeepSeek's flexibility opens up opportunities for creating innovative solutions across industries.

Chapter 7: Real-World Use Cases and Case Studies

In this chapter, we will explore how industries across the globe are leveraging DeepSeek's powerful AI models to drive innovation, boost productivity, and create cutting-edge solutions. Through detailed case studies and success stories, we will highlight how businesses and organizations are using DeepSeek in healthcare, education, marketing, and other sectors to enhance efficiency and outcomes. Additionally, we will discuss key lessons learned from these real-world applications, providing valuable insights for others looking to implement DeepSeek in their operations.

Case Studies from Industries Benefiting from DeepSeek

1. Healthcare: Enhancing Patient Care and Research Efficiency

DeepSeek is making waves in healthcare by assisting medical professionals in improving patient care, accelerating research, and managing complex data sets. Hospitals and medical research organizations are using DeepSeek's AI capabilities to analyze patient records, identify medical trends, and even predict future health outcomes.

- **Example Case Study: AI-Powered Diagnostic Assistant** A leading healthcare provider integrated DeepSeek into their diagnostic workflow to analyze patient data, medical images, and historical records. Using DeepSeek's deep learning models, they were able to develop an AI-powered assistant that helped doctors diagnose diseases such as cancer, heart conditions, and rare illnesses more quickly and accurately. By processing large datasets, DeepSeek's AI could highlight patterns and anomalies that were difficult for human doctors to spot, reducing diagnostic errors and improving patient outcomes.
- **Impact:**
  - Enhanced diagnostic accuracy by 25%.
  - Reduced the time spent on patient evaluations by 30%.
  - Streamlined administrative workflows, allowing healthcare workers to focus more on patient interaction.
- **Lesson Learned:** The key takeaway from this implementation was the importance of training DeepSeek's models with high-quality, diverse datasets. This helped

ensure that the AI's diagnostic suggestions were reliable and relevant across various patient demographics.

---

2. Education: Revolutionizing Learning and Student Support

DeepSeek is helping educational institutions innovate by enabling personalized learning experiences, automating administrative tasks, and providing real-time support to students. Schools, universities, and ed-tech companies are adopting AI-driven solutions to improve learning outcomes, tailor educational content, and manage large amounts of academic data.

- **Example Case Study: Personalized Learning Assistant in Schools** An educational technology company used DeepSeek to develop a personalized learning assistant that could analyze student performance, identify learning gaps, and offer tailored educational resources. By integrating DeepSeek into their platform, they provided real-time feedback to students and helped teachers identify areas where students were struggling. DeepSeek's natural language processing (NLP) capabilities allowed the system to understand the context of student responses, enabling it to offer nuanced suggestions for improvement.

- **Impact:**
  - Increased student engagement by 40%.
  - Improved student retention rates through targeted interventions.
  - Reduced teacher workload by automating administrative tasks such as grading and progress tracking.
- **Lesson Learned:** A critical lesson from this project was the importance of continuously updating DeepSeek's models with fresh, relevant educational content to ensure that the assistant could remain aligned with evolving curriculum standards and student needs.

---

3. Marketing: Automating Content Creation and Customer Insights

In the marketing industry, DeepSeek is transforming how businesses create content, engage with customers, and analyze market trends. By utilizing AI-driven tools for data analysis, content generation, and customer segmentation, marketers can make data-driven decisions that enhance brand visibility and customer loyalty.

- **Example Case Study: Automated Content Generation for Digital Marketing Campaigns** A global marketing agency leveraged DeepSeek to automate content creation for social media campaigns, blog posts, and email newsletters. By inputting target keywords and content parameters into DeepSeek's model, the agency generated high-quality, SEO-optimized content in a fraction of the time it would have taken a human team. Additionally, DeepSeek's AI was used to analyze customer feedback and generate insights on customer preferences, enabling the agency to craft personalized campaigns that resonated with specific audience segments.
- **Impact:**
  - Reduced content creation time by 50%.
  - Increased website traffic by 20% due to improved SEO.
  - Boosted customer engagement with personalized, relevant content.
- **Lesson Learned:** One valuable takeaway was the importance of monitoring the output of DeepSeek's AI to ensure that the generated content remains authentic and

aligns with brand voice and values. While DeepSeek's capabilities are impressive, human oversight is essential for maintaining quality control.

Exploring How Businesses Are Using DeepSeek for Productivity Enhancements

DeepSeek's AI models are not only used for creating new products or services but also for improving internal processes and productivity. Here are some examples of how businesses are using DeepSeek to enhance efficiency within their teams:

1. Automating Customer Support with AI Chatbots

A customer support center for an e-commerce company implemented DeepSeek's chatbot model to handle routine inquiries, order status checks, and product recommendations. By automating these common tasks, the company freed up human agents to focus on more complex customer issues.

- **Impact:**
    - Reduced response times for customer queries by 60%.

- Increased customer satisfaction due to 24/7 availability.
- Allowed human agents to handle more specialized cases, improving overall efficiency.

---

2. Streamlining Data Analysis for Business Intelligence

A financial services firm used DeepSeek to automatically analyze market trends, generate reports, and identify investment opportunities based on historical data. By integrating DeepSeek's data analysis capabilities, the firm could process large volumes of financial data more quickly and with greater accuracy.

- **Impact:**
  - Reduced the time spent on data analysis by 40%.
  - Improved decision-making by providing real-time insights into market conditions.
  - Enabled the company to respond more quickly to changes in market trends.

Success Stories and Lessons Learned from Real-World Applications

Throughout these case studies, several key takeaways have emerged that can help businesses ensure the successful implementation of DeepSeek's AI models.

1. Data Quality Is Key

Whether you're working with healthcare data, educational records, or customer feedback, the quality of the data you feed into DeepSeek's models directly impacts the performance of the AI. Ensuring that your data is clean, well-organized, and representative of real-world scenarios is crucial for achieving accurate and actionable results.

2. Start Small and Scale

For businesses new to AI implementation, it's often wise to start with smaller, less complex use cases. This allows you to fine-tune DeepSeek's models and processes before scaling them to handle larger datasets or more critical tasks.

3. Collaboration Is Essential

DeepSeek's open-source nature means that developers, data scientists, and industry experts can collaborate to refine models and share best practices. Collaboration with other stakeholders can accelerate the implementation process and ensure that the AI is optimized for specific industry needs.

Conclusion

DeepSeek is already transforming industries by enhancing productivity, automating tasks, and providing valuable insights. Through the case studies and success stories shared in this chapter, it's clear that DeepSeek's models can drive significant improvements in sectors such as healthcare, education, marketing, and more. As businesses continue to adopt AI, the lessons learned from these real-world applications will help others navigate the integration process and maximize the potential of DeepSeek to achieve their goals. In the next chapter, we will explore future trends and innovations in AI that will further shape the landscape of industries using DeepSeek.

Chapter 8: The Future of DeepSeek and AI

In this chapter, we will look ahead to the future of DeepSeek and its role in shaping the next generation of artificial intelligence. By analyzing emerging trends in AI and exploring DeepSeek's potential developments, we will highlight the direction in which the platform is headed, its opportunities for innovation, and how it will continue to contribute to the broader AI ecosystem.

The Potential Future Developments for DeepSeek

DeepSeek has already made significant strides in advancing the capabilities of AI, but its journey is far from over. The platform is expected to evolve further, introducing new features and models that will drive even greater value across various industries. Key developments to watch for include:

1. Expansion of Multimodal Capabilities

DeepSeek's ability to handle multiple types of data—such as text, images, and audio—sets it apart from many AI models. However, this capability is still in its early stages. Future updates to DeepSeek will likely include the integration of more sophisticated multimodal functionalities, enabling the platform to process even more complex data types simultaneously.

- **Example:** Future iterations of DeepSeek could allow businesses to analyze video data in real-time, pulling insights from both visual and auditory cues. This could have major applications in sectors like media, entertainment, and security.

2. Enhanced Natural Language Understanding (NLU)

While DeepSeek already boasts impressive natural language processing (NLP) abilities, future versions are expected to deepen its understanding of context, tone, and sentiment in more nuanced ways. By improving its grasp of human emotions, intent, and conversational subtleties, DeepSeek could enhance its use in customer service, virtual assistants, and other areas that require sophisticated human-AI interaction.

- **Example:** Imagine a future DeepSeek-powered virtual assistant that can fully understand and react to the emotional state of a user, providing responses that are not only factually accurate but also emotionally intelligent, thus delivering a more personalized user experience.

3. Autonomous AI Models

A potential future development for DeepSeek is the introduction of more autonomous AI models. These models could be capable of learning and adapting to new tasks with minimal human input, becoming increasingly efficient as they gather more data and experiences. This would allow DeepSeek to be used in a wider range of industries and applications, including autonomous driving, predictive maintenance, and real-time decision-making in high-stakes environments.

- **Example:** In the logistics industry, DeepSeek could potentially power fully autonomous systems that handle inventory management, predictive shipping, and even route optimization without human intervention.

4. Advanced Customization Options for Users

Another promising development for DeepSeek is enhancing its customization capabilities. Currently, users can adjust settings and fine-tune the platform's models for specific tasks. Future updates may allow even deeper customization, enabling users to create personalized AI workflows and bespoke applications tailored to unique business needs.

- **Example:** Future versions of DeepSeek could allow users to "train" the models with their own proprietary datasets, resulting in highly specialized AI solutions for industries like finance, retail, or agriculture.

How DeepSeek Fits into the Larger AI Landscape

DeepSeek plays a pivotal role in the broader AI ecosystem, especially as the open-source AI movement continues to grow. By making powerful AI tools accessible and customizable for developers, businesses, and individuals, DeepSeek contributes to the democratization of AI, ensuring that advanced technology is no longer the sole domain of large corporations and tech giants.

1. Open-Source AI Movement

DeepSeek is at the forefront of the open-source AI revolution, where the focus is on collaboration and transparency. Open-source platforms like DeepSeek allow users to modify, adapt, and improve the underlying code, leading to a more diverse and innovative ecosystem. As more companies and individuals contribute to the platform, DeepSeek's capabilities will grow exponentially, creating a collective pool of knowledge that benefits everyone.

- **Example:** As part of the open-source community, DeepSeek allows developers to share models, contribute to updates, and build upon existing code to create more advanced AI tools. This fosters innovation and leads to faster advancements in AI technology.

2. Interoperability with Other AI Solutions

One of the critical ways DeepSeek fits into the larger AI landscape is by focusing on interoperability. Future versions of DeepSeek are likely to enhance their ability to seamlessly integrate with other AI models, platforms, and software solutions. This ensures that businesses can combine the best of multiple AI tools to solve complex challenges.

- **Example:** Businesses may choose to integrate DeepSeek's capabilities with other popular AI solutions, such as TensorFlow, PyTorch, or IBM Watson, to build more sophisticated systems that incorporate features from multiple models.

Emerging Trends in AI and Where DeepSeek Is Headed

The AI industry is rapidly evolving, and several emerging trends will shape the future of platforms like DeepSeek. In this section, we'll explore some of the most exciting trends in AI and how DeepSeek is positioned to capitalize on them.

1. AI Ethics and Responsible AI

As AI continues to influence more aspects of daily life, concerns around AI ethics are growing. The focus is shifting toward creating responsible AI systems that are fair, transparent, and unbiased. DeepSeek's open-source nature provides an ideal foundation for addressing these ethical concerns, as the community can collaborate to ensure that the AI models remain aligned with ethical guidelines and standards.

- **Example:** Future developments of DeepSeek may include tools for auditing AI decisions, identifying biases in training data, and ensuring that the models respect privacy and confidentiality in sensitive applications, such as healthcare or finance.

2. AI for Sustainability

The role of AI in addressing global challenges such as climate change, energy consumption, and sustainable agriculture is becoming more prominent. DeepSeek could play a critical role in helping organizations adopt sustainable practices by providing AI tools that optimize resource usage, minimize waste, and reduce environmental impact.

- **Example:** DeepSeek might be used in smart grid systems to optimize energy distribution, in agriculture to optimize water usage, or in supply chains to reduce carbon footprints by predicting and minimizing inefficiencies.

3. AI-Driven Creativity and Content Generation

AI is increasingly being used in creative industries to assist with content generation, from art to music to writing. DeepSeek's ability to generate high-quality content can revolutionize industries like marketing, media, and entertainment, where the demand for fresh, engaging content is constant. In the future, DeepSeek's AI could become an essential tool for artists, writers, and content creators looking to generate innovative works at scale.

- **Example:** Future versions of DeepSeek could be used to generate unique visual artwork, write scripts for films or advertisements, or even assist in composing original music for various media productions.

4. AI-Powered Autonomous Systems

Autonomous systems powered by AI are expected to become more widespread in the coming years. DeepSeek's development towards autonomous learning and decision-making will allow it to be applied to industries such as transportation, logistics, manufacturing, and more. DeepSeek's AI-driven models will be able to optimize processes in real-time, reducing human error and improving overall system efficiency.

- **Example:** DeepSeek could be applied in autonomous vehicles, where AI models predict traffic patterns, optimize driving routes, and enhance safety protocols without human intervention.

Conclusion

The future of DeepSeek is exciting and filled with opportunities. As the platform continues to evolve, we can expect it to push the boundaries of what AI can do, offering increasingly sophisticated models that serve a wide range of industries. From enhanced customization to deeper multimodal capabilities, DeepSeek is poised to be a key player in the AI ecosystem for years to come. By staying aligned with emerging trends in AI and contributing to the open-source movement, DeepSeek will continue to shape the future of innovation and efficiency across various sectors.

Chapter 9: Ethical Considerations and Data Privacy

As artificial intelligence (AI) continues to become an integral part of industries and daily life, the ethical use of AI and data privacy concerns have gained significant attention. In this chapter, we will explore the key ethical considerations surrounding the use of DeepSeek, the AI platform, and examine how its technology impacts user data privacy. By understanding these concerns, users can ensure they interact with DeepSeek responsibly while adhering to best practices in data handling.

Exploring the Ethical Use of AI Models

AI models like DeepSeek have immense potential to drive innovation and solve complex problems across various industries. However, with great power comes great responsibility. Ethical concerns are integral to the design, deployment, and use of AI models. This section will cover some of the critical ethical issues related to AI models like DeepSeek.

1. AI Bias and Fairness

AI models are trained on data, and if that data is biased or unrepresentative, the AI may inherit and amplify those biases. This can lead to unintended discriminatory outcomes in applications like hiring, lending, or law enforcement. DeepSeek, like any other AI model, must be evaluated for fairness, ensuring that it does not perpetuate existing biases or discriminate against certain groups.

- **Example:** When using DeepSeek for job applicant screening, the model must be tested to ensure it does not show bias based on factors such as gender, ethnicity, or socioeconomic background. Ethical AI development focuses on identifying and addressing such biases during the training process.

2. Transparency and Explainability

AI decision-making is often seen as a "black box," where the logic behind an AI's decisions is not easily understood by humans. Ensuring transparency and explainability in DeepSeek's AI models is critical to building trust with users and stakeholders.

- **Example:** A healthcare provider using DeepSeek for medical diagnosis should be able to explain how the AI arrived at a specific conclusion. This is particularly important when AI recommendations have serious consequences, such as treatment decisions or legal outcomes.

3. Accountability in AI Decisions

As AI models become more autonomous, questions about accountability emerge. When an AI system makes a decision, who is responsible if something goes wrong? Ethical AI practices advocate for clear lines of accountability, ensuring that there are mechanisms in place to address any adverse outcomes caused by AI decisions.

- **Example:** In the case of DeepSeek being used in autonomous vehicles, if an AI model makes a decision that results in an accident, determining who is accountable—whether it's the developer, the user, or the platform provider—is an essential ethical concern.

4. Human Oversight

While DeepSeek can be a powerful tool, human oversight remains crucial. The role of human decision-makers is indispensable in ensuring AI operates within ethical boundaries and aligns with societal values.

- **Example:** When DeepSeek is used for customer service automation, a human operator should be able to review the AI's responses, particularly in sensitive or complex cases, to ensure that the automated system's decision-making aligns with company values and ethical standards.

Understanding Data Privacy Concerns and Policies in Using DeepSeek

Data privacy is one of the most pressing concerns in the AI industry, especially as AI systems, like DeepSeek, process vast amounts of personal and sensitive information. Ensuring that users' data is handled responsibly and securely is critical to maintaining trust in DeepSeek's platform.

1. Types of Data Collected by DeepSeek

DeepSeek's models, depending on the use case, may collect and process different types of data, such as:

- **Personal Information:** Data like names, email addresses, and phone numbers when users register on the platform.
- **Interaction Data:** Data generated during interactions with DeepSeek's models, including inputs and outputs, may be stored for model improvement.

- **Behavioral Data:** Information about user interactions with the DeepSeek platform, such as usage patterns and preferences.

It is important to know what data DeepSeek collects and how it is used to ensure that users' privacy is respected.

2. Data Anonymization and Encryption

To mitigate privacy risks, data anonymization and encryption techniques are critical. DeepSeek must ensure that personally identifiable information (PII) is anonymized when it is used for training models or analytics. Additionally, all sensitive data should be encrypted both in transit and at rest, preventing unauthorized access or data breaches.

- **Example:** If DeepSeek collects data for training purposes, user information should be anonymized so that individual identities cannot be traced back to the original data. Encryption ensures that this anonymized data remains secure.

3. User Consent and Transparency

DeepSeek should adhere to transparent data collection practices, informing users about what data is being collected, why it is needed, and how it will be used. Users should provide explicit consent before their data is processed, especially when using DeepSeek in personalized or sensitive contexts.

- **Example:** When using DeepSeek for content generation or customer support tasks, users should be made aware of how their data is used to improve the model and should have the option to opt out of data collection if desired.

4. Data Retention and Deletion Policies

Data retention policies must define how long user data is stored and under what circumstances it will be deleted. DeepSeek should give users control over their data, including the ability to delete personal data from the platform or opt out of data collection at any time.

- **Example:** DeepSeek should provide users with clear instructions on how to delete their account and associated data. If users choose to no longer use the platform, their data should be permanently deleted after a set period of time unless otherwise required for legal or operational reasons.

5. Compliance with Regulations

DeepSeek must comply with global data privacy laws and regulations, such as the **General Data Protection Regulation (GDPR)** in the European Union, the **California Consumer Privacy Act (CCPA)** in the United States, and other regional privacy laws. This includes providing users with access to their data, the ability to correct inaccuracies, and the ability to withdraw consent.

- **Example:** DeepSeek must ensure that users in the EU have the right to access, correct, or delete their personal data, as mandated by GDPR. Similarly, users in California should have the right to opt out of data sharing under CCPA guidelines.

Best Practices for Handling User Data Responsibly When Interacting with DeepSeek Models

To promote responsible data handling, users and developers must adhere to best practices when using DeepSeek. These best practices will help safeguard privacy and ensure ethical use of data:

1. Implement Privacy by Design

From the outset, ensure that data privacy is an integral part of the AI development and deployment process. This includes anonymizing data, ensuring secure access controls, and building transparency into the system.

- **Example:** As a developer integrating DeepSeek into an application, you should implement privacy controls in your app, such as user data consent forms and options for users to manage their data preferences.

2. Regular Data Audits

Conduct regular audits of the data collected by DeepSeek to ensure that it is being used responsibly and complies with data privacy policies. This includes reviewing how data is stored, accessed, and deleted.

- **Example:** DeepSeek's data usage practices should be reviewed annually by internal or external auditors to ensure they comply with privacy regulations and ethical guidelines.

3. Educate Users about Data Privacy

Educating users about data privacy best practices is essential. Ensure that users understand how their data will be used, how they can control their data, and how to protect their privacy when interacting with DeepSeek.

- **Example:** Provide users with clear documentation on the types of data collected, how it is used, and the security measures in place to protect their information. Transparency about data handling fosters trust.

Conclusion

Ethical considerations and data privacy are foundational elements in the responsible development and use of AI systems like DeepSeek. By addressing concerns around bias, transparency, accountability, and privacy, users and developers can ensure that DeepSeek remains a trustworthy and impactful AI platform. As AI technology continues to evolve, it is essential that we remain vigilant in our efforts to uphold ethical standards and protect user data, fostering an environment where AI is used for the benefit of society as a whole.

Chapter 10: Troubleshooting and Common Issues

While DeepSeek is designed to provide powerful AI solutions, like any technology, users may encounter issues from time to time. This chapter addresses some of the most common problems users face when working with DeepSeek, offers practical solutions for resolving them, and provides guidance on optimizing performance for different environments. Additionally, we'll explore available community support channels to help users get the assistance they need.

Common Problems Users Face and How to Resolve Them

In this section, we'll look at several typical issues that users may encounter when interacting with DeepSeek's models and how to troubleshoot or resolve them effectively.

1. Slow Response Times

One of the most common problems users face is slow or delayed response times when interacting with DeepSeek. This can occur for several reasons, including network issues, server overload, or insufficient system resources.

Solution:

- **Check Internet Connection:** Ensure that you have a stable and fast internet connection, as a weak or intermittent connection can cause delays.
- **Reduce Model Complexity:** If you're running a heavy or complex model, try simplifying the prompt or reducing the model size to speed up processing.
- **Check Server Status:** Visit DeepSeek's server status page (if available) to check for any ongoing maintenance or server outages.
- **Upgrade System Resources:** If running DeepSeek locally, ensure that your system meets the minimum hardware requirements for the model. Upgrading RAM or CPU power can help improve performance.

2. Model Output Is Unclear or Unintended

Another common issue is receiving responses or outputs from DeepSeek that are unclear, irrelevant, or do not meet expectations. This is often a result of incorrect input or an ineffective prompt.

Solution:

- **Refine Input Prompts:** Ensure that your input is clear and well-defined. For example, asking very general questions can lead to vague or unhelpful answers. Use more specific instructions or questions.

- **Provide Context:** Give the model more context about the task you want it to perform. For example, when using DeepSeek for content generation, provide details about the tone, style, and intended audience.
- **Iterate and Experiment:** AI models may not always get things perfect on the first try. Don't hesitate to iterate and experiment with different variations of your prompt until you get the desired results.

3. Compatibility Issues Across Platforms

Users may experience compatibility issues when trying to run DeepSeek on different devices, such as iOS, Android, or on web interfaces. Some features may not work properly across all platforms or versions of the app.

Solution:

- **Update the App:** Make sure you are using the latest version of the DeepSeek app, as updates often fix compatibility issues and introduce new features.
- **Check Platform Requirements:** Verify that your device meets the minimum system

requirements for DeepSeek, especially if you're running the app on mobile devices.
- **Clear Cache and Reinstall:** If you're experiencing issues with the app, try clearing the cache or reinstalling the app to resolve any corrupted files or settings.

4. API Integration Failures

For developers working with DeepSeek through APIs, integration failures can occur due to incorrect configurations, outdated libraries, or incompatibilities with other software.

Solution:

- **Check API Documentation:** Ensure that you're following the latest API documentation provided by DeepSeek. API endpoints and authentication methods may change over time.
- **Use Debugging Tools:** Use debugging tools or logs to trace errors and identify where the problem lies in the code.
- **Verify API Limits:** Be aware of any rate limits or usage quotas for API requests. Exceeding these limits may cause the API to fail or return error codes.
- **Contact Developer Support:** If you encounter persistent issues, reach out to

DeepSeek's developer support team for assistance.

5. Insufficient System Resources When Running Locally

Running DeepSeek locally, especially for larger models, can demand significant computational resources. If you're running into issues such as crashes or slow performance, it could be due to insufficient CPU, RAM, or storage.

Solution:

- **Increase Available Resources:** Consider upgrading your hardware if running DeepSeek locally for more resource-intensive tasks. At a minimum, ensure that you meet the system requirements for optimal performance.
- **Use Cloud Resources:** If local resources are insufficient, consider running DeepSeek on cloud platforms like AWS, Google Cloud, or Microsoft Azure, which provide scalable computing power.
- **Close Unnecessary Applications:** Free up system resources by closing other applications that are not essential for running DeepSeek.

Optimizing Performance for Different Environments

DeepSeek can be used across various environments, from personal desktops and laptops to mobile devices and cloud-based servers. Each environment presents its own set of challenges and opportunities for optimization.

1. Optimizing DeepSeek for Local Environments

When running DeepSeek locally, performance can be heavily influenced by your computer's hardware, system settings, and network conditions. Here's how to optimize for a smoother experience:

- **Use Lightweight Models:** If your system has limited resources, opt for lighter versions of DeepSeek's models that offer faster performance without sacrificing too much accuracy.
- **Maximize RAM Usage:** Ensure that your system's memory is being fully utilized. Close unnecessary programs that are consuming memory and preventing DeepSeek from operating at full capacity.
- **Use Multi-Threading:** If your system supports multi-threading, configure

DeepSeek to take advantage of multiple CPU cores for faster model processing.

2. Optimizing DeepSeek for Cloud Environments

Cloud platforms offer scalability and flexibility, but performance can still vary depending on the configuration and resources allocated. Here are a few tips for optimizing DeepSeek on cloud services:

- **Choose the Right Instance Type:** Select cloud instances that offer adequate CPU and GPU resources for your needs. For AI tasks, instances with powerful GPUs (such as NVIDIA Tesla or A100) can significantly boost performance.
- **Optimize Storage:** Ensure that your cloud storage is optimized for fast data retrieval. Use SSDs instead of HDDs for quicker loading times.
- **Monitor Resource Utilization:** Use monitoring tools provided by the cloud platform to track CPU, memory, and network usage to ensure you're not under- or over-provisioning resources.

3. Optimizing DeepSeek for Mobile Environments

Running DeepSeek on mobile devices can be challenging due to the limited computational resources of smartphones and tablets. Here's how to optimize the experience:

- **Use Mobile-Friendly Models:** Choose smaller, more efficient models that are optimized for mobile processing.
- **Optimize Battery Usage:** Use DeepSeek in moderation to prevent excessive battery drain. Many mobile apps have built-in power-saving modes that can help extend battery life.
- **Ensure Adequate Internet Speed:** Mobile devices are often dependent on Wi-Fi or cellular data. Make sure you have a stable and fast internet connection to avoid delays or interruptions.

Community Support and Where to Find Help

While troubleshooting can resolve many issues, sometimes users may need additional assistance. DeepSeek's vibrant community and robust support resources can help users find solutions to problems they can't solve on their own.

1. DeepSeek's Official Support Channels

DeepSeek provides several official support channels to help users get the help they need:

- **Knowledge Base:** DeepSeek's knowledge base is an excellent resource for troubleshooting common issues, understanding new features, and exploring FAQs.
- **Help Desk:** If you can't find the solution in the knowledge base, you can submit a support ticket to DeepSeek's help desk team, who will assist you with more complex issues.
- **Email Support:** DeepSeek provides email support for users experiencing specific technical difficulties. Reach out to their support team for personalized troubleshooting assistance.

2. Community Forums

DeepSeek has an active online community where users can share experiences, ask questions, and find answers. Join forums to participate in discussions and learn from others.

- **User Forums:** DeepSeek's user forums allow you to post questions, share tips, and troubleshoot issues with fellow users.

- **Reddit and Other Social Media Groups:** Many users discuss DeepSeek's models on platforms like Reddit, Discord, and Facebook. These platforms can be a great place to ask for help or exchange ideas with the broader DeepSeek community.

3. Tutorials and Online Courses

If you're encountering issues due to a lack of experience with DeepSeek's features, online tutorials and courses can help you better understand how to use the platform.

- **YouTube Channels:** Many creators offer in-depth tutorials on using DeepSeek for various use cases.
- **Online Learning Platforms:** Websites like Udemy, Coursera, and LinkedIn Learning may offer courses that teach you how to integrate and troubleshoot DeepSeek in different environments.

Conclusion

Troubleshooting issues with DeepSeek can often be a matter of understanding the platform's functionality and addressing underlying technical problems. Whether you're facing slow response times, API integration issues, or performance challenges in different environments, this chapter has provided solutions and tips to help you overcome common obstacles. Additionally, with the support of DeepSeek's community and official resources, you have the tools to quickly resolve problems and ensure an optimal user experience.

CHAPTER 11: DeepSeek-V3: The Next Evolution in AI Technology

Introduction to DeepSeek-V3

DeepSeek-V3 is the latest iteration of DeepSeek's AI models, incorporating significant advancements that redefine the potential of artificial intelligence in both performance and application. Building on the foundations of previous versions, DeepSeek-V3 introduces new features that enable users to tackle more complex tasks, generate more accurate insights, and integrate AI into diverse platforms with greater ease. This chapter explores the core features, enhancements, and use cases of DeepSeek-V3, making it clear why it's set to revolutionize industries across the board.

---

1. What is DeepSeek-V3?

DeepSeek-V3 is a powerful, next-generation AI model designed to handle sophisticated tasks across multiple domains. With a primary focus on natural language processing (NLP), multimodal inputs, real-time data analysis, and scalable performance, DeepSeek-V3 sets itself apart from earlier versions through its ability to process and respond faster, more accurately, and in a more human-like manner.

Key Features:

- **Superior NLP Capabilities**: Enhanced understanding of natural language, including regional dialects and specialized jargon.
- **Multimodal Functionality**: Ability to work with text, images, and videos in a unified context.
- **Real-Time Performance**: Optimized for faster processing, making it ideal for time-sensitive tasks.
- **Customizable Models**: The option to fine-tune models for specific industries or use cases.

---

2. Improvements in Natural Language Processing (NLP)

DeepSeek-V3 builds on its natural language capabilities by offering a more nuanced understanding of context, tone, and intent in conversations. Unlike previous versions, V3 has a deep contextual memory that allows it to engage in longer conversations while maintaining coherence.

New NLP Features:

- **Advanced Sentiment Analysis**: Understanding emotions and tone in conversations, providing contextually aware responses.
- **Contextual Memory**: DeepSeek-V3 can retain information over the course of multiple interactions, making it ideal for personalized user experiences.
- **Multilingual Understanding**: Support for a broader range of languages and dialects, including regional variants, to cater to a global audience.

---

3. Multimodal Capabilities: Text, Images, and Video

One of the most groundbreaking features of DeepSeek-V3 is its ability to handle multimodal inputs simultaneously. This means users can provide both textual and visual information, and DeepSeek will generate more comprehensive responses that integrate both.

Multimodal Use Cases:

- **Text and Image Processing**: The ability to describe and generate captions for images, process visual content with text, and offer insights based on both modalities.

- **Video Analysis**: DeepSeek-V3 can now watch and interpret videos, identifying key elements, summarizing content, and generating descriptions.
- **Integrated Outputs**: Create content that combines text, images, and videos in a cohesive manner, ideal for creative industries such as marketing and content creation.

---

4. Faster Processing and Real-Time Performance

DeepSeek-V3 is engineered for speed, allowing users to get results almost instantly. This makes it ideal for applications that require quick feedback, such as customer service bots, live data analysis, or real-time content generation.

Speed Improvements:

- **Real-Time Data Processing**: Instantaneous responses to user queries, even with complex data inputs.
- **Optimized for Edge Devices**: DeepSeek-V3 runs efficiently on lower-powered devices without sacrificing performance, making it accessible for all types of users.

- **Scalability**: From small businesses to large enterprises, DeepSeek-V3 scales to meet the demands of both small-scale and high-demand environments.

---

5. Customization and Tailored Outputs

DeepSeek-V3 takes AI customization to the next level, allowing users to adjust the model to better fit their specific needs. Whether you're looking for a more creative response or more technical accuracy, DeepSeek-V3 can adapt to provide exactly what you require.

Customization Options:

- **Model Fine-Tuning**: Customize DeepSeek-V3 for specific tasks or industries, such as healthcare, finance, or entertainment.
- **Response Parameters**: Adjust key parameters such as tone, creativity, or verbosity to match your desired output style.
- **API Integration**: DeepSeek-V3 offers a robust API that enables seamless integration with existing applications, allowing for real-time interactions and data processing.

---

6. API and Developer Support

DeepSeek-V3 comes with an enhanced API that offers developers greater flexibility and ease of integration. The API allows for embedding DeepSeek's powerful AI capabilities into a wide range of applications, from mobile apps to enterprise software.

Developer Benefits:

- **Enhanced API Capabilities**: Integration with multiple platforms, including web, mobile, and desktop applications.
- **Detailed Documentation**: Comprehensive guides and examples that make integration straightforward for developers, even those new to AI.
- **Cross-Platform Support**: DeepSeek-V3 can be embedded across multiple devices and operating systems, ensuring compatibility with your existing tools.

---

7. Security and Privacy Enhancements

As AI technology continues to evolve, it is critical to maintain a strong focus on user data security and ethical considerations. DeepSeek-V3 introduces new privacy features to ensure that user data is protected and used responsibly.

Security Features:

- **End-to-End Encryption**: All data processed by DeepSeek-V3 is securely encrypted to prevent unauthorized access.
- **Ethical AI Practices**: DeepSeek-V3 is built to adhere to ethical guidelines, ensuring that its use does not contribute to harmful biases or misinformation.
- **Data Privacy Control**: Users can control how their data is used, with transparency about data storage, processing, and sharing.

---

8. Real-World Applications of DeepSeek-V3

DeepSeek-V3 has already made waves in a variety of industries, showcasing its versatility and potential to solve real-world problems. Here are just a few areas where DeepSeek-V3 is having an impact:

- **Healthcare**: Assisting with diagnostics by analyzing medical images and patient data to suggest potential diagnoses.
- **Education**: Providing personalized tutoring experiences, answering student queries in real-time, and generating educational content.

- **Marketing**: Generating creative content, analyzing customer sentiment, and automating personalized marketing campaigns.
- **Customer Support**: Offering real-time, intelligent responses to customer inquiries, reducing wait times, and enhancing satisfaction.

---

9. Looking Ahead: The Future of DeepSeek-V3

The future of DeepSeek-V3 is bright, with further enhancements on the horizon. As AI technology continues to evolve, DeepSeek will likely expand into even more specialized applications, offering more tailored solutions to businesses and consumers alike.

Future Developments:

- **Continued Multimodal Innovation**: DeepSeek-V3's ability to process a variety of data types will continue to improve, with more advanced image and video processing capabilities.
- **Smarter Personalization**: DeepSeek's contextual memory and learning algorithms will become more intelligent, offering even deeper personalization options.

- **Integration with IoT**: Future updates may enable DeepSeek-V3 to work with Internet of Things (IoT) devices, enabling smarter homes and offices.

Conclusion

DeepSeek-V3 is not just an upgrade; it's a revolution in AI technology. With enhanced performance, multimodal capabilities, real-time processing, and customization options, DeepSeek-V3 sets the stage for a wide range of industries to adopt and benefit from AI. As it continues to evolve, its impact on both business and everyday life will only grow, solidifying its place as one of the most advanced and versatile AI tools available today.

CHAPTER 12: How to Install and Run DeepSeek-V3

Installing and running DeepSeek-V3 can vary depending on your preferred platform (Windows, macOS, Linux, or cloud). In this guide, we'll walk through the steps for setting up DeepSeek-V3 on your local machine and through cloud services for greater scalability. This installation includes all prerequisites, step-by-step procedures, and tips to help you get started quickly.

Prerequisites

Before you begin, make sure you have the following:

1. **Basic understanding of command-line operations.**
2. **A supported operating system** (Windows, macOS, or Linux).
3. **Python** installed (preferably Python 3.7+).
4. **Git** installed for cloning repositories.
5. **An internet connection** for downloading dependencies and models.

Step 1: Downloading DeepSeek-V3

Option 1: Installing via GitHub Repository (for Local Installation)

1. **Clone the Repository**:
    - Open your terminal or command prompt and navigate to the directory where you want to install DeepSeek-V3.
    - Run the following command to clone the DeepSeek-V3 GitHub repository:

      ```
      bash
      CopierModifier
      git clone
      https://github.com/deepseekai/DeepSeek-V3.git
      ```

    - This will download the DeepSeek-V3 files to your local machine.
2. **Navigate to the Project Directory**:
    - Change to the newly created directory:

      ```
      bash
      CopierModifier
      cd DeepSeek-V3
      ```

3. **Set up a Virtual Environment (Optional but Recommended)**:
    - Set up a virtual environment to isolate your installation from other Python projects:

      ```
      bash
      CopierModifier
      ```

python -m venv deepseek_env
source deepseek_env/bin/activate #
On macOS/Linux
deepseek_env\Scripts\activate # On
Windows

4. **Install Dependencies**:
   - Install the necessary dependencies by running:

     bash
     CopierModifier
     pip install -r requirements.txt

Option 2: Using Docker (For Consistency Across Environments)

1. **Install Docker**: Ensure Docker is installed on your machine. You can download Docker from here.
2. **Pull the DeepSeek-V3 Docker Image**:
   - Pull the latest DeepSeek-V3 Docker image by running:

     bash
     CopierModifier
     docker pull deepseekai/deepseek-v3

3. **Run DeepSeek-V3 in Docker**:
   - After the image is pulled, run the following command to start the DeepSeek-V3 container:

```bash
CopierModifier
docker run -p 5000:5000
deepseekai/deepseek-v3
```

4. This will expose DeepSeek-V3 via a local port on your machine.

Step 2: Running DeepSeek-V3 Locally

Once the installation is complete, you can interact with DeepSeek-V3 through the command line or a web interface (if enabled).

Option 1: Command Line Interface (CLI)

1. **Run the DeepSeek-V3 CLI**:
   - Navigate to the project directory and run DeepSeek-V3 via the command line:

     ```bash
     CopierModifier
     python deepseek_v3.py
     ```

2. **Interact with DeepSeek-V3**:
   - Once the model is running, you can use the command line to input prompts or interact with the model by specifying tasks. For example:

```bash
CopierModifier
python deepseek_v3.py --input "What is the weather like in New York?"
```

3. **Review Output**: The model will process the request and return a response, which you can interact with further.

Option 2: Web Interface (if Available)

1. **Launch the Web Interface**:
    - If you are running DeepSeek-V3 on your local machine with a web interface, simply open a web browser and go to:

      ```arduino
      CopierModifier
      http://localhost:5000
      ```

    - This will open DeepSeek-V3's interface, where you can input tasks and view outputs in a more user-friendly format.
2. **Interact with the Interface**:
    - Type in prompts or commands directly into the provided text field.
    - DeepSeek-V3 will process the input and provide responses directly in the web browser.

Step 3: Integrating DeepSeek-V3 into Your Applications

Once DeepSeek-V3 is running locally, you can integrate it into your applications via the API.

1. **Access the API**:
   - If you're running DeepSeek-V3 on a local server (via Docker or the command line), you can make HTTP requests to interact with it. The API should be available at:

     bash
     CopierModifier
     http://localhost:5000/api/v1/perform_task

2. **Sending API Requests**:
   - Use POST requests to send data to DeepSeek-V3 and receive results. Here's an example of how to send a request using Python's requests library:

     python
     CopierModifier
     ```
     import requests
     ```

```
url =
"http://localhost:5000/api/v1/perfo
rm_task"
data = {"task": "Translate 'Hello' into
Spanish"}
response = requests.post(url,
json=data)
print(response.json())
```

3. This will send a task to the DeepSeek-V3 model and print out the response.

Step 4: Cloud-Based Deployment (Optional)

For users looking to scale and access DeepSeek-V3 on the cloud, you can deploy it to services like AWS, Google Cloud, or Azure. The process typically involves:

1. **Containerizing DeepSeek-V3** using Docker.
2. **Uploading the Docker image** to the cloud service.
3. **Configuring the cloud server** to run DeepSeek-V3 in a scalable environment.

Refer to specific cloud service documentation for detailed steps on deploying Docker containers.

Troubleshooting

- **Issue: Model not starting or freezing on startup**
  - Solution: Ensure that all dependencies are installed properly using pip install -r requirements.txt. Check for any missing libraries.
- **Issue: Slow response times**
  - Solution: Ensure your system meets the hardware requirements (particularly for GPU usage). If you're running it on a cloud-based platform, consider increasing the instance size or adding GPUs for faster processing.
- **Issue: API calls return errors**
  - Solution: Check the API documentation for correct request formats and ensure that DeepSeek-V3 is running at the specified URL.

Conclusion

With these steps, you should be able to install and run DeepSeek-V3 on your local machine or cloud-based environment. By following the setup guide and leveraging the power of DeepSeek-V3, you'll be able to integrate advanced AI capabilities into your workflows and applications. Whether you're using it for content generation, customer service, or real-time analysis, DeepSeek-V3 offers the flexibility and performance needed to solve complex problems efficiently.

Glossary

1. **DeepSeek** – An open-source AI model known for its high efficiency and versatility in various applications such as content creation, data analysis, and customer support.
2. **DeepSeek-V3** – The latest version of the DeepSeek AI model, featuring enhanced performance, advanced features, and expanded capabilities over previous iterations.
3. **AI Model** – A computational system that uses data and algorithms to simulate human intelligence, enabling systems like DeepSeek to perform tasks such as language processing, image recognition, and decision-making.
4. **DeepSeek API** – An application programming interface that allows developers to integrate DeepSeek's AI functionalities into their own applications for seamless automation and intelligence.
5. **DeepSeek Integration** – The process of embedding DeepSeek's AI models into other software systems or workflows, facilitating automation and improved efficiency.
6. **DeepSeek Installation** – The process of setting up DeepSeek or DeepSeek-V3 on a device or cloud infrastructure, ensuring the AI model can run and be utilized effectively.
7. **DeepSeek Setup** – The steps required to configure DeepSeek models for specific tasks, platforms, or environments, including hardware and software prerequisites.
8. **DeepSeek-R1** – A version of the DeepSeek model focused on core AI tasks, providing a more lightweight but powerful solution for standard applications.

9. **DeepSeek-V3 Setup** – The process of preparing and configuring DeepSeek-V3 specifically, enabling its advanced features and customizations for user needs.
10. **Machine Learning (ML)** – A subset of artificial intelligence where DeepSeek models are trained to recognize patterns in data and make predictions or decisions based on it.
11. **Open-Source AI** – AI models like DeepSeek that are freely available for modification, distribution, and use, allowing the community to contribute to their development and improvement.
12. **DeepSeek API Key** – A unique identifier required for accessing DeepSeek's API, enabling developers to securely interact with the AI system.
13. **DeepSeek for Developers** – The usage of DeepSeek models by developers to create customized applications, leveraging AI for data processing, automation, and other tasks.
14. **DeepSeek AI Capabilities** – The specific abilities of DeepSeek models, including natural language processing, image recognition, and predictive analytics, that make them suitable for diverse applications.
15. **DeepSeek Cloud Deployment** – Hosting and running DeepSeek models on cloud infrastructure to ensure scalability and accessibility for businesses and developers.
16. **DeepSeek Customization** – Modifying DeepSeek or DeepSeek-V3's settings, parameters, and workflows to meet specific business or user requirements.
17. **DeepSeek Performance Tuning** – Optimizing DeepSeek-V3 for faster processing, reduced latency, and better efficiency, especially for high-demand applications.

18. **Data Privacy with DeepSeek** – Ensuring the secure handling of sensitive user data when interacting with DeepSeek AI models, especially in compliance with regulations like GDPR.
19. **DeepSeek Security** – Features and protocols in DeepSeek models designed to protect against unauthorized access, cyberattacks, and data breaches.
20. **DeepSeek Use Cases** – Specific scenarios or industries in which DeepSeek AI models are applied, such as content creation, customer support, healthcare, and marketing.
21. **DeepSeek-V3 Features** – The key characteristics of DeepSeek-V3, including improved accuracy, multi-platform support, and enhanced API capabilities.
22. **AI Automation with DeepSeek** – Using DeepSeek to automate tasks, workflows, and processes, saving time and increasing productivity in various industries.
23. **DeepSeek Data Analysis** – The use of DeepSeek's advanced algorithms to process and analyze large datasets for insights, trends, and decision-making.
24. **DeepSeek Multimodal AI** – A feature of DeepSeek-V3 that allows the AI model to process and integrate multiple types of data, such as text, images, and audio, for more comprehensive solutions.
25. **DeepSeek Scalability** – The ability of DeepSeek to handle large volumes of data and complex tasks across various systems and environments, including cloud platforms and distributed networks.

Conclusion: Embracing the Future of AI with DeepSeek

As we conclude this comprehensive guide on DeepSeek, it's important to reflect on the key takeaways and the potential that DeepSeek holds for both individuals and businesses looking to harness the power of open-source AI.

Key Takeaways About DeepSeek

- **Powerful Open-Source AI**: DeepSeek-V3 represents a significant step forward in the world of artificial intelligence, offering cutting-edge, open-source models that provide high efficiency, scalability, and cost-effectiveness. Whether you are a developer, a business owner, or an individual looking to leverage AI, DeepSeek makes it possible to tap into advanced AI capabilities without breaking the bank.
- **Versatile Models and Customization**: With models like DeepSeek-R1 and DeepSeek-VL, users can tackle a wide range of applications—from natural language processing to multimodal tasks. The ability to customize and integrate these models into various environments gives users

flexibility and control over their AI implementations.

- **Seamless Integration**: Whether you're working with DeepSeek via mobile apps, web interfaces, or APIs, the platform makes it easy to get started and dive deep into powerful AI tools. Its cross-platform compatibility ensures that you can work efficiently no matter where you are or what device you're using.
- **Growing Community and Support**: The open-source nature of DeepSeek fosters a community of innovators, developers, and AI enthusiasts who share their knowledge and collaborate on solving challenges. The availability of tutorials, forums, and expert support ensures that you're never alone on your AI journey.

Encouraging Continued Exploration of Open-Source AI Tools

DeepSeek is only one example of the vast potential that open-source AI holds for the future. The flexibility of open-source models allows businesses, developers, and individual users to explore, innovate, and contribute to the evolution of AI in ways that were once reserved for large corporations with massive resources.

The open-source community continues to thrive and grow, providing opportunities for everyone—from hobbyists to industry professionals—to take advantage of these tools. By participating in this movement, you can help shape the future of AI technology, contribute to the creation of new models, and even build upon existing systems to solve unique challenges in your field.

Final Thoughts on the Impact of DeepSeek and AI Innovations on the Future of Work and Technology

The advent of AI tools like DeepSeek-V3 is transforming the way we work and interact with technology. From improving productivity and streamlining business processes to enabling entirely new ways of solving complex problems, AI's role in the future of work is undeniable.

In particular, open-source AI models like DeepSeek democratize access to powerful technologies, allowing individuals and smaller organizations to compete on a level playing field with larger enterprises. As AI becomes more integrated into daily operations, it will drive further innovation across industries such as healthcare, education, marketing, and beyond.

The future of AI is bright, and innovations like DeepSeek are just the beginning. As the landscape of technology continues to evolve, the potential for AI to empower both individuals and businesses is limitless. Whether you're looking to enhance your personal skills, build the next great AI-powered tool, or contribute to the ongoing development of these technologies, now is the time to explore, experiment, and embrace the possibilities that AI offers.

DeepSeek's journey is one of many in the rapidly evolving field of AI. Its impact on both the future of technology and the future of work will only continue to grow, bringing about profound changes in how we approach problems, create solutions, and connect with one another in an increasingly digital world.

DeepSeek-V3 represents a significant advancement in the world of open-source AI models, offering a powerful and flexible solution for businesses, developers, and AI enthusiasts alike. With its improved capabilities, integration features, and seamless usability across multiple platforms, DeepSeek-V3 provides users with the tools to unlock innovative applications, streamline workflows, and enhance productivity.

Whether you are looking to harness its potential for content creation, data analysis, customer support, or integrating advanced AI into existing systems, DeepSeek-V3 empowers users to achieve more with AI. The ease of setup, coupled with its scalability in cloud environments, ensures that DeepSeek-V3 is accessible to users of all levels—whether you're just getting started or are a seasoned developer.

By continuously evolving and pushing the boundaries of what open-source AI can do, DeepSeek-V3 positions itself as a versatile and valuable tool for a wide range of use cases. As AI continues to shape the future of work and technology, DeepSeek-V3 is set to play a key role in driving innovation and efficiency in industries worldwide.

As we look to the future, the continued development and support for DeepSeek-V3 will likely open new doors to even more groundbreaking capabilities, ensuring that it remains at the forefront of the AI revolution. With its growing community and open-source nature, the possibilities for DeepSeek-V3 are vast, and its impact on the AI landscape is poised to be lasting.

By embracing open-source AI tools like DeepSeek, you are not just exploring powerful technology—you are becoming part of a larger movement that is shaping the future of AI and its applications across the globe. Now is the time to continue your exploration, experiment with new ideas, and unlock the transformative potential of AI in your own work and projects.

Appendices

A1: How to Install and Run DeepSeek-R1 on Different Platforms

This appendix provides step-by-step instructions on how to install and run the DeepSeek-R1 model on various platforms to ensure users can leverage its capabilities regardless of their operating system or device.

Installing on Web (Browser-based)

1. Visit the official DeepSeek website.
2. Create an account or sign in.
3. Navigate to the models section and select DeepSeek-R1.
4. Follow the on-screen instructions to start using the model directly in your browser.
   - No installation required—just log in and begin your exploration!

Installing on iOS and Android (Mobile App)

1. **For iOS:**
   - Open the App Store on your device.
   - Search for the DeepSeek app.
   - Tap "Install" and follow the prompts.
   - Once installed, log in to access DeepSeek-R1.
2. **For Android:**

- Go to the Google Play Store.
- Search for the DeepSeek app.
- Tap "Install" and follow the setup steps.
- Log in to begin using DeepSeek-R1 directly from your mobile device.

Running DeepSeek-R1 Locally (For Developers)

1. Ensure you have Python 3.x and the necessary dependencies installed on your computer.
2. Download the DeepSeek-R1 package from the official GitHub repository or DeepSeek website.
3. Extract the files to a directory of your choice.
4. Open a terminal or command prompt, navigate to the extracted folder, and install the necessary dependencies using:

   ```
   pip install -r requirements.txt
   ```

5. Once installed, run DeepSeek-R1 using the following command:

   ```
   python deepseek_r1.py
   ```

6. The model will now be up and running locally, and you can interact with it as needed.

A2: Glossary of AI-Related Terms

This glossary provides clear definitions of commonly used AI-related terms to help readers better understand the technical aspects discussed in the book.

- **AI (Artificial Intelligence)**: The simulation of human intelligence in machines programmed to think and learn.
- **Model**: An algorithm that has been trained on data to make predictions or decisions without explicit programming.
- **Machine Learning (ML)**: A type of AI where models learn from data and improve over time without being programmed with specific instructions.
- **Deep Learning**: A subset of machine learning that uses neural networks with many layers to analyze various forms of data.
- **Natural Language Processing (NLP)**: A field of AI focused on the interaction between computers and human language.
- **API (Application Programming Interface)**: A set of protocols and tools for building software applications, allowing one program to interact with another.
- **Open-Source**: Software whose source code is available for modification and distribution by anyone.

- **Training Data**: The data used to train AI models, helping them learn and make accurate predictions.
- **TensorFlow**: An open-source library used for machine learning and deep learning tasks, often used to develop AI models.
- **Neural Network**: A computing system inspired by the way biological neural networks in the human brain work, crucial for deep learning.

A3: Resources for Further Learning

For those interested in deepening their understanding of AI and maximizing the potential of DeepSeek, the following resources will be helpful:

1. **DeepSeek Official Resources**:
   - **Website**: www.deepseek.ai - Official website for model documentation, downloads, and tutorials.
   - **GitHub Repository**: DeepSeek GitHub - Access the source code, updates, and open-source projects.
   - **Community Forum**: DeepSeek Forum - A place to ask questions, share knowledge, and engage with the community.
2. **Online Learning Platforms**:
   - **Coursera**: AI for Everyone - A beginner-friendly course introducing the basics of AI.
   - **Udacity**: Intro to Machine Learning with PyTorch - An in-depth course on machine learning and deep learning with practical examples.
   - **edX**: Artificial Intelligence Courses - A wide range of AI-related courses from top universities.
3. **Books and Articles**:

- *"Deep Learning with Python"* by François Chollet - A great resource for understanding deep learning concepts.
- *"Hands-On Machine Learning with Scikit-Learn, Keras, and TensorFlow"* by Aurélien Géron - Offers practical, hands-on examples using popular AI tools and libraries.
- Articles from **Medium**: Deep Learning at Medium - Read insightful articles on AI, deep learning, and the latest trends.

4. **AI Communities and Forums**:
   - **Stack Overflow**: AI Tag - A community for technical Q&A and troubleshooting.
   - **Reddit**: r/MachineLearning - A hub for AI and machine learning discussions and news.
   - **AI Alignment Forum**: AI Alignment - Explore the ethical aspects of AI and how to align models with human values.

By leveraging these resources, you can continue your journey into the exciting world of AI and make the most of DeepSeek's powerful open-source capabilities.

Table of Contents

www.ingramcontent.com/pod-product-compliance
Lightning Source LLC
La Vergne TN
LVHW022351060326
832902LV00022B/4372

* 9 7 9 8 3 0 8 8 3 0 2 4 5 *